SIMPLE TRICKS FOR HEALTHY LIFE

SIMPLE WAYS TO LIVE HEALTHY

Ryan Stones.

TABLE OF CONTENTS

INTRODUCTION

Being healthy involves more than just getting in shape and feeling great; it also involves maintaining that state.

Maintaining good physical health might also help you maintain good mental health. Your body will be strong if you eat the correct foods and exercise regularly. This will help you deal with stress and ward off disease. Healthy eating and regular exeexercise when you're a teen will also help you maintain good health as you get older.

PHYSICAL ACTIVITY

To maintain and enhance health, physical activity is crucial. Although the human body was created to move, modern lives make it harder than ever to be active throughout the day. Despite the fact that one in two persons in the United States has a chronic disease, just half of adults in the country obtain the recommended amount of exercise each day. Regardless of sex, colour, ethnicity, or current fitness level, staying physically active can have significant advantages at every stage of life.Regardless of your understanding of what exercise is or

isn't, the fact remains that exercise involves movement. It doesn't matter if you stroll around the block or run a marathon; any movement is exercise, and it counts every time you move more than you usually do.

Many reasons why you shouldn't. It could be that you're too busy, unsure of where to begin, unmotivated, or concerned that you'll be hurt. You might believe that working out needs to be extremely difficult or that it must be of poor quality.

ADVANTAGES OF EXERCISE

Exercise has both short-term and long-term positive effects on a person's physical and mental health, whether they are healthy, at risk of acquiring chronic diseases, or already have a chronic condition or disability. Regular exercise improves sleep quality and lowers blood pressure and anxiety in the near term. It can improve one's disposition, offer one more energy, and allow one to enjoy time with friends and family.

Regular exercise has advantages that go beyond calorie balancing and weight maintenance. The benefits of physical activity for health are numerous:

- **Reduced chance of premature death**
- **Reduced risk of stroke, type 2 diabetes, hypertension, and cardiovascular disease**
- **Better cholesterol**
- **Improved muscular strength, endurance, and aerobic capacity**

- **Promotes Better brain function and cognition**

Additionally, it has been demonstrated that regular exercise improves digestion and delays the natural aging-related drop in metabolism. Lean muscle mass can be maintained with exercise, and more calories can be expended even while sedentary since inactive fat stores are replaced with active lean muscle mass.

Additionally, it has been demonstrated that exercise increases insulin sensitivity, which helps to maintain appropriate blood sugar levels.

To maximize the health advantages of exercise, it is vital to mix up your activity:

a. Stretching: for example, makes movement easier, increases flexibility, and guards against muscle tension and injury. Additionally, stretching aids in the body's pre-exercise warming up.

b. Balance: Exercises that test your stability will help you keep a good posture and prevent falls.

c. Strength or Weight Training: Strength or weight training builds bone strength, improves balance, and increases muscular mass. Both

at home and in a gym, one can perform strength training.

d. Aerobic or cardiovascular exercise: Aerobic exercises strengthen the heart and lungs, boost endurance, reduce body fat, and enhance circulation. Aerobic exercises include running, walking, cycling, stair climbing, dancing, and swimming.

EATING HEALTHY

Consuming a range of foods from all 5 major food categories in the suggested serving sizes constitutes healthy eating.

Eating a variety of foods from the five main food groups keeps your diet interesting with a diversity of flavors and textures while also supplying your body with a variety of nutrients, promoting overall health, and maybe lowering your risk of disease.

Many of the items that are frequently consumed on a daily basis in modern diets do not fall within one of the five food groups. These items, also known as "junk" or "occasional foods," can be eaten occasionally but shouldn't be a regular part of a healthy diet. Oils and fats High kilocalorie foods are essential for a balanced diet. Whatever your starting point, it's simple to make small adjustments to align your eating with the healthy lifestyle you seek. Just concentrate on consuming foods from the five major food

groups while cutting back on infrequent foods.

Taking Baby Steps to Develop Healthier HabitsPeople are frequently driven to lose weight by discomfort with their present weight or recurring health issues. Small adjustments have a significant impact on both weight loss and general health. Rarely do significant changes happen over night. Your daily eating choices might help you transition to a healthy lifestyle.

To lose weight, follow these few simple steps:

- **Maintain a food diary. Over the course of a year, eating too many calories might cause weight gain. Every bite should count, so pay attention to portions.**

- **To lower your risk of disease and to boost your health, walk for 45 to 60 minutes.**

- **Having a nutritious breakfast helps you avoid nibbling later in the day.**

- **Fruits, carrots, and low-fat yogurt are wise options for quelling hunger in between meals.**

- **The drinks you choose matter a lot.**

  The total daily caloric intake is influenced by beverage selections. Drinks can be beneficial, but you should be wary of the empty-calorie, which can considerably increase your daily caloric intake.

Since beverages make up a significant portion of what kids eat during this crucial developmental period, research indicates that what kids drink from birth to age 5 can have a significant impact on their health. Plain water for hydration and plain pasteurized milk for nutrition are now suggested by medical professionals. the limit It is advised to consume 100° juice in moderation and to limit or prohibit the addition of sugar to beverages.Limit your intake of sodium.

High blood pressure, a risk factor for cardiovascular disease, is exacerbated by an excess of sodium. Make sure the majority of your diet is fresh and unprocessed because packaged and processed foods can have shockingly high salt contents.

LIMIT HARMFUL FAT

Your chance of developing disease is increased by saturated and trans fats, which can boost your low-density lipoprotein (LDL) cholesterol. Limit your consumption of fried foods, processed meats, red meat, and pastries to avoid these fats.

Substitute monounsaturated and fats, which are present in foods like olive oil, avocado, almond, cashews, salmon, and anchovies, for these.

Make healthier decisions now. A healthier lifestyle can be improved with small, everyday improvements. Keep a food diary for a week to get started, then review it to check if a range of items from the food groups are present. Some people find that just writing down what they eat and drink helps them make good decisions.

MENTAL HEALTH

The subject of mental health is hot right now, and for good reason. The National Alliance on Mental Illness reports that 1 in 5 adults had mental illness in 2018, and that 16.5 percent of children and adolescents aged 6 to 17 had a mental health issue in 2016. Anxiety, depression, attention deficit hyperactivity disorder, and post-traumatic stress disorder are the

most common mental health conditions. According to experts, mental illnesses are becoming more widespread. It is crucial to investigate both the relationship between mental health and physical health as well as the function of healthy eating habits in the management of mental health issues as medical practitioners and researchers attempt to understand these conditions and discover effective therapies.

EFFECT OF MENTAL HEALTH ON GENERAL HEALTH.

A general definition of health is "a condition of being free from disease and/or illness and characterized by physical, mental, and social well-being." In other words, good health encompasses everything. It includes regular exercise, enough sleep, a balanced diet, and social interactions. Basic health-promoting behaviors improve life quality and may lower the risk of developing chronic illnesses.

Physical and mental health are interdependent, and studies have shown that mental health disorders are linked to the development, control, and risk of diseases like diabetes, hypertension, stroke, heart disease, and cancer as well as to their treatment and progression. Chronic health problems frequently come before mental health disorders, whereas the symptoms of mental health disorders are exacerbated by chronic illnesses. This loop makes it more difficult to cure or recover from either problem.

SLEEP

A person's overall health and wellness, quality of life, and safety—both on the road and at work—can all be significantly impacted by how much sleep they receive or don't get. According to the Centers for Disease Control and Prevention, at least 15 out of every 30 days, 25% of American adults do not get enough sleep or rest. Unknown many, this loss of sleep has a more significant effect on health.

ADVANTAGES OF SLEEP

Getting enough good quality sleep has several advantages.

Sleep helps the body fight off disease, supports the metabolism of sugar to fend off diabetes.

Can enhance academic achievement, and increases productivity and safety at work, in addition to making one feel rested and alert.

It can also lessen the chance of developing chronic illnesses. Each day getting adequate sleep can enhance overall health and enjoyment.

For most adults, at least seven hours of sleep each night is needed for proper cognitive and behavioral functions. An insufficient amount of sleep can lead to serious repercussions. Some studies have shown sleep deprivation leaves people vulnerable to attention lapses, reduced cognition, delayed reactions, and mood shifts.

It's also been suggested that people can develop a sort of tolerance to chronic sleep deprivation. Though their brains and bodies struggle due to lack of sleep, they may not be aware of their own deficiencies because less sleep feels normal to them.

SLEEP AND HUNGER

The connection between sleep and hormone regulation can help to explain some of the detrimental effects sleep has on chronic illnesses and weight gain. The body creates hormones that aid in regulating hunger, energy metabolism, and glucose processing while you sleep. Lack of sleep is associated with increased ghrelin levels, decreased leptin levels, and increased insulin synthesis after meals. These three hormones control glucose levels, encourage fat storage, signal the brain when it has received enough food, and increase hunger.

The overproduction or underproduction of these hormones is harmful for maintaining a healthy weight.

RECOMMENDATION FOR SLEEP

The American Academy of Sleep Medicine and the Sleep Research Society issued a joint consensus statement as a result of research into the quantity of sleep required to reap the advantages of appropriate rest. These organizations recommend that individuals (18+ years) usually sleep seven or more hours each night for best health. In addition to good quality, proper timing and regularity, and the absence of sleep disruptions and disorders, healthy sleep is often measured by duration. Young individuals, those who are unwell, or those who are recuperating from partial or complete sleep deprivation may also need

nine hours or more of sleep per night. Children's sleep needs are very different from adults' sleep needs.

The importance of getting enough sleep during adolescence is gaining national attention. Despite the recommendation to sleep for eight to ten hours per night, the Centers for Disease Control and Prevention and the American Academy of Pediatrics report that nearly 70% of teenagers sleep for seven hours or less on a school night. Because of how bad the phenomenon is, high school start times should be pushed back in order to better accommodate teenagers' biological clocks. Lack of sleep

frequently causes people to forgo breakfast, which is crucial for teenage development.

THE BEST WAYS TO SLEEP

Professionals concur that there are easy actions you may do to begin improving your sleep:

- Reduce your caffeine intake after noon.
- Get frequent exercise, but avoid it three hours before bed.
- Unwind and get some rest in a screen-free atmosphere.

Solutions needs to be particular to a person's sleep requirements. A challenge for one individual may not be for another.

It's crucial to recognize individual sleeping patterns and issues, and to seek outside assistance if necessary.

Along with physical exercise, with good sleep and eating practices, create the groundwork for lifetime wellness and general health.

www.ingramcontent.com/pod-product-compliance
Lightning Source LLC
LaVergne TN
LVHW052110160826
845678LV00015B/3472